WILDLIFE WORLDS

ASIA

Tim Harris

W

FRANKLIN WATTS

LONDON • SYDNEY

Franklin Watts
First published in Great Britain in 2019 by The Watts Publishing Group
Copyright © The Watts Publishing Group, 2019

HB ISBN: 978 1 4451 6733 6
PB ISBN: 978 1 4451 6734 3

Printed in Dubai

FSC
www.fsc.org

MIX
Paper from
responsible sources
FSC® C104740

Series Editor: Amy Pimperton
Series Designer: Nic Davies smartdesignstudio.co.uk
Picture researchers: Rachelle Morris (Nature Picture Library),
Laura Sutherland (Nature Picture Library), Diana Morris

Picture credits:
Dreamstime:Agami Photo Agency 3b,7b; Carl99 back cover tcl,16-17c; Nico Smit 21b.
Nature PL: Aflo 2b, 13b, 26-27c; Franco Banfi 8, 19cr; Gertrud & Helmut Denzau 23tr; Hanne &
Jens Eriksen 29tr, 29c; David Fleethan 9b; Nick Garbutt front cover b; Edwin Giesbers front cover t;
Sergey Gorshkov 6c,7t; Graeme Guy/BIA 25tr; Alex Hyde 10-11b; Olga Kamenskaya 18bl, 19br; Tim
Laman 21tr; Valeriy Maleev 15c,15b; Gavin Maxwell 27tl; Konstantin Mikhailov 15tl; Constantinos
Petrinos 9tl; David Pike 12c; Michael Pitts 16b; Fiona Rogers 11tr; Andy Rouse 24c, 24bl; Roland
Seitre 17tr; Markus Varesvuo 13tl; Theo Webb 25b; Staffan Widstrand 27tr.
Shutterstock: Zakirov Aleksey 3t, 18-19c; brnitat 23; brsbw18 17; Butterfly Hunter 6t;Dmussman
1,13tr, 32b; David Evison 11br; ExOrzist back cover tr; frantisekhojdysz backcover tc, 2t,9tr; Andrei
Gilbert 19bc; Yann Hunbert 6b; Daniel Karflik 3bg, 4-5bg,14, 31bg; Louie Lea 28c; Wang LiQuang
19tr; Phil MacDPhoto 27bl,32t; Matulee 5; Mazur Travel: 4c,11tc,30b; Meoita 29br; Mirinae front
cover c; Tom B Payne 29bl;Dmitry Pichugin 15tr; Meet Podar 21tl; Ondrej Prosicky 4b; Ais Qocak
23tc;Matyas Rehak 20, 31c; Andreas Rose 27br; Salparadis back cover tl, 11tl;Signature Message
3c, 17bl; Vladimir Wrangel 21c, 23cr, 30t; Andrea Zangrilli 22-23c;Milan Zygmunt 25tl.
CC Wikimedia Commons/Peeliden 12.

Franklin Watts
An imprint of
Hachette Children's Group
Part of The Watts Publishing Group
Carmelite House
50 Victoria Embankment
London EC4Y 0DZ
An Hachette UK Company

www.hachette.co.uk
www.franklinwatts.co.uk

With thanks to the Nature Picture Library

Contents

Asian Continent

Stretching from the Arctic Ocean in the north to the Indian Ocean in the south, and from the Ural Mountains in the west to the Pacific Ocean in the east, Asia is the largest of all the continents. It is also the most varied. There is frozen tundra in Siberia, tropical rainforest in Malaysia, Indonesia and Thailand, and a vast desert on the Arabian Peninsula.

Asia also has vast areas of grassland, called steppes, mangrove forests, wetlands, huge cave systems, and coral reefs. With such a range of environments, it is little wonder that the plant and animal life of the continent is also varied. Many animals, including tigers, South Asian river dolphins, giant pandas and Asian elephants live wild only in Asia.

The corpse lily is found on the islands of Sumatra and Borneo.

BENGAL TIGER

Both of Asia's longest rivers – the Yangtze (6,300 kilometres) and the Yellow (5,464 kilometres) – are in China.

At 8,848 metres, Mount Everest in the Himalayas is the highest mountain in the highest mountain range in the world.

Giant pandas live in bamboo forests in the mountains of China. They spend most of their time eating bamboo.

ARCTIC OCEAN

ARCTIC CIRCLE

RUSSIA

RUSSIA

EUROPE

Ural Mountains

Lake Baikal

Khongoryn Els

Kamchatka Peninsula

SEA OF OKHOTSK

Tolbachik volcanoes

CASPIAN SEA

Caucasus Mountains

Gobi Desert

YELLOW RIVER

JAPAN

Himalayas

CHINA

Mount Fuji

Ranthambore

YANGTZE RIVER

South China Karst (Guilin)

Arabian Desert

GANGES RIVER

INDIA

PACIFIC OCEAN

Arabian Peninsula

Al Hajar Mountains

Sundarban Mangroves

BAY OF BENGAL

AFRICA

ARABIAN SEA

THAILAND

PHILIPPINES

Tubbataha Reef

MALAYSIA

Borneo Rainforest

EQUATOR

Sumatra

INDONESIA (WHICH INCLUDES THOUSANDS OF ISLANDS)

The Dead Sea Depression is 413 metres below sea level.

INDIAN OCEAN

Kamchatka Peninsula

In the far east of Russia, the Kamchatka Peninsula is a mountainous land of snow-capped volcanoes that sits between the mighty Pacific Ocean and the Sea of Okhotsk.

Wildlife is abundant, with brown bears roaming the tundra, woodlands and meadows. Lynx, foxes, wolves and sables hunt hares and rodents, such as marmots and lemmings. Thousands of seabirds nest on coastal cliffs, feeding on fish from the ocean, where there are whales, dolphins and seals.

Kamchatka is known as the 'land of fire and ice' for a good reason. It is the most volcanic part of Asia and 29 of its 160 volcanoes – including the Tolbachik volcanoes (above) – are active. The region is bitterly cold for much of the year and the landscape is covered with snow and ice.

The rare spoon-billed sandpiper sweeps its unique, spatulate bill through the water from side-to-side as it feeds.

Sleek sables are related to weasels and otters. They spend most of their time in the branches of trees.

Humpback whales dive up to 200 metres underwater in search of krill and small fish.

In winter, Steller's sea eagles hunt for fish from the sea ice that floats on the water.

Tubbataha Reef

To the west of the islands of the Philippines, the Tubbataha Reef system was discovered in the 1970s. It is now known to be one of the most remarkable in the world.

SEA FAN

The reef is a kaleidoscope of colour, with more than 350 different kinds of hard and soft coral (including sea fans) and almost 500 types of fish – including the endangered Napoleon wrasse. Sharks and sea turtles visit in search of a meal. There are two coral atolls where the reef breaks the water's surface. This is where seabirds nest on beaches of white sand.

NAPOLEON WRASSE

The greater blue-ringed octopus is no bigger than a golf ball, but has a deadly venomous bite. When threatened, the rings on its skin flash bright blue as a warning to predators.

Among the many creatures that visit the reef are hammerhead sharks. Their wide-set eyes give them 360 degrees of vision.

9

Borneo Rainforest

Although many of its trees have been cut down for their valuable wood, one of the world's oldest rainforests covers much of Asia's largest island – Borneo. Large parts of the rainforest are unexplored.

More than 3,000 different kinds of tree make up the forest, some of them growing 50 metres tall. They provide a home for an astonishing variety of animals, many of which live nowhere else. There are apes, monkeys, rhinos, elephants, clouded leopards, squirrels and bats. Hundreds of kinds of bird and amphibian live here, and thousands of insects.

The forest is very thick. Fallen trees and thick, tangled vines make it hard for a person to walk through it. Colourful butterflies flit though glades, hornbills fly from tree to tree in search of fruit and at dusk, flying foxes flap above the canopy, where orangutans munch on leaves.

Huntsman spiders rest on trees. From here they ambush insect prey.

The corpse lily is named for its disgusting smell. The smell attracts flies, who help with pollination. Its flower is the largest of any plant – up to 1 metre across.

Orangutans are the most solitary of the great apes. Highly intelligent, they build nests of branches and leaves high in trees in which to sleep.

Large, fruit-eating rhinoceros hornbills have a hollow casque on their beak. It helps to amplify their calls.

Mount Fuji

At 3,776 metres, this dormant volcano is the highest peak in Japan. It features very strongly in Japanese culture and tradition and is one of the country's 'holy mountains'.

Fuji's higher slopes are barren and often covered with snow, but the lower slopes are cloaked in broadleaved and coniferous forest. Black bears, Japanese serows (goat-antelopes) and foxes live in the forest. In spring it echoes to the sound of birdsong.

The Japanese emperor butterfly is the national butterfly of Japan.

Pine nuts are a spotted nutcracker's favourite food, which is why this bird lives in conifer trees.

Often unafraid of people, Japanese macaques are both intelligent and bold. In winter they warm themselves in hot volcanic pools.

In spring, the cherry blossom on the lower slopes of Mount Fuji is spectacular and a favourite food of Japanese macaques. The cherry trees are in full bloom in mid-April.

Gobi Desert

Northern China and southern Mongolia host the largest desert in Asia – the Gobi. It is so dry because it is in the rain shadow of the high Tibetan Plateau to the south. On a summer's day it may be hot, but at night the temperature often plunges well below freezing.

Much of the Gobi is bare rock, with cliffs and steep-sided canyons. Other areas are grassy or covered with thickets of saxaul shrubs. Although the environment is waterless, sometimes baking hot and sometimes bitterly cold, many animals cope with the conditions. Camels, gazelles and even snow leopards live here.

There are some massive sand dunes in the Gobi Desert, such as the Khongoryn Els, which are 180 kilometres long and 300 metres high. They are known as *Duut Mankhan* or 'Singing Dunes', for the sound the sand makes as the wind blows it.

Wild onions are a food source for many grazing animals.

A Bactrian camel has a distinctive double hump. This type of camel is very rare in the wild as most are domesticated.

Jerboas hop fast on long hind legs. They have excellent hearing and their big ears help them lose heat on hot days.

By day, long-eared hedgehogs rest in burrows they have dug or taken over from other animals. They come out to feed on insects and lizards at night.

South China Karst

When rain and river water dissolve limestone bedrock, it creates an amazing landscape called karst. The city of Guilin in southern China is famous for its karst formations.

Water has shaped limestone that is more than 300 million years old into pinnacles, rock bridges, cliffs and canyons. Huge caves carry underground rivers. Many different kinds of animal live in the caves and nowhere else. They include fish, bats and cave crickets. Above ground, a variety of animals make their home in the forests.

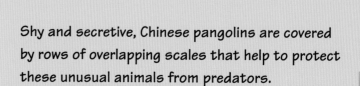

Shy and secretive, Chinese pangolins are covered by rows of overlapping scales that help to protect these unusual animals from predators.

Rock towers and cones rise 300 metres above the plain like giants' teeth. Incredibly, trees grow on the near-vertical cliff faces.

Great roundleaf bats roost alone or in small groups in caves. They use echolocation to hunt insects at night.

Although Asian golden cats climb well, they spend most of their time on the ground.

Male long-tailed silver pheasants have striking plumage.

Lake Baikal

There is more water in Russia's Lake Baikal than in all North America's Great Lakes combined. Not only is it the largest freshwater lake on Earth (by volume), it also the deepest, plunging to 1,642 metres. Its surface waters freeze each winter.

The clear waters of this ancient lake are home to many fish, including golomyankas, which thrive even at the greatest depths. There are also seals, water birds, crustaceans, freshwater snails and even sponges. Surrounding the lake is conifer forest, where brown bears, wolves, elk, wild boar and chipmunks live.

BAIKAL SPONGE

Lake Baikal first formed in a deep rift valley, where Earth's crust was pulling apart, more than 25 million years ago. The lake increases in width by about 2 centimetres every year.

Every year, Siberian rubythroats return to the area around the lake to breed. They leave for their winter quarters in Southeast Asia in September.

Many of the crustaceans found here, such as this amphipod, are native to Lake Baikal.

Baikal black grayling swim in shallow water close to the lake's shore.

Baikal seals bask on the shores of the lake when they are not fishing in its waters.

Sundarban Mangroves

On the vast delta of the Ganges and Brahmaputra rivers, straddling the border between Bangladesh and India, is the world's largest mangrove forest, the Sundarbans.

The coming together of the Bay of Bengal's saltwater with the fresh river water has created a place of extraordinary diversity. Crocodiles, turtles and fish swim in the creeks and kingfishers perch overhead, looking for unsuspecting fish. Mongooses, fishing cats and chital deer feed in the dense mangroves, where an apex predator – the Bengal tiger – hunts stealthily.

Unlike most trees, mangroves are tolerant of the salty seawater that floods the delta's creeks and channels at every high tide.

Thousands of people are bitten by the venomous common krait every year. These snakes are often found close to water sources.

When the tide is low, fiddler crabs scuttle across the muddy margins of creeks.

Fishing cats sometimes dive into water to catch fish. They can swim long distances and can even swim underwater.

Chital deer rest in the shade during the hottest part of the day. They come out to feed in the early morning and evening when it is cooler.

Ganges River

The mighty Ganges River carries snowmelt from its glacial source in the Himalaya Mountains, monsoon rain from the Indian plains and water from countless tributaries, large and small.

After a journey of over 2,500 kilometres, the river passes through the world's largest delta to the Bay of Bengal. Deer, wild boar and jackals come to its banks to drink, where they are watched by crocodiles on the lookout for a meal. Otters, turtles and snakes swim in its waters, while herons wade carefully through the shallows, ready to dart forward and grab a passing fish. Kites constantly soar overhead.

More water flows to the ocean from the Ganges than from any other river apart from the Amazon and the Congo. Hindus consider the river to be sacred. It supports millions of people and an astonishing variety of wildlife, including endangered gharials.

Brahminy kites are 'housekeepers', eating dead fish and crabs that litter the side of the river.

Only a few hundred gharials survive in the Ganges. These long-snouted crocodiles only eat fish.

Spotted pond turtles swim in search of snails and insect larvae to eat.

After a fishing expedition, an Oriental darter holds its wings spread out to dry them.

Ranthambore

Once a place where the wealthy maharajas (princes) of Jaipur hunted tigers, Ranthambore, in India, is now a national park where these big cats are protected.

With a mixture of broadleaved forest, grassland, wetlands and many lakes, the park is an exceptional place for wildlife. Tigers are the main attraction, but there are also leopards, hyenas, macaques, crocodiles, snakes and more than 300 kinds of bird, including thousands of water birds.

BENGAL TIGER

Tigers hunt in the forest surrounding the ruins of Ranthambore fort. It is described as 'dry' forest because it receives rain only during the monsoon.

Mugger crocodiles eat any animal they can get their jaws around, whether alive or dead.

White-throated kingfishers dive into water for fish. Both males and females have this spectacular plumage. Their distinctive call sounds a little like laughter.

A male Indian peafowl, or peacock, with its tail spread is an amazing sight.

Himalayas

The Himalayas is the highest mountain range in the world, with more than 50 peaks topping 7,200 metres. They run 2,300 kilometres from Bhutan in the east to northern Pakistan.

MOUNT EVEREST

High in the mountains, hundreds of glaciers carry ice down deep, steep-sided valleys below barren summits. Thousands of fast-flowing rivers tumble over rocks, with pools providing homes for fish and water birds. At lower altitudes, meadow grasses and wildflowers grow on mountain slopes in spring and summer. Lower still, the grassland is replaced by forest, the home of bears, deer and many other animals.

The Himalayan jumping spider lives at altitudes up to 6,700 metres. It is possibly one of the highest-dwelling animals on Earth.

Feeding on bone marrow from the skeletons of dead animals, the lammergeier (or bearded vulture) has a most unusual diet for a bird of prey.

In spring, Himalayan blue poppies flower in high meadows.

Snow leopards live solitary lives on rocky mountain slopes above the tree line. Their fur markings help these wild cats blend into the landscape.

Al Hajar Mountains

Hot, almost lifeless desert covers most of the Arabian Peninsula, but more rain falls in the Al Hajar Mountains of Oman, allowing plants and animals to thrive.

Jebel Shams is the highest peak in the Al Hajar Mountains, rising to just over 3,000 metres. It overlooks a deep canyon. From its slopes are spectacular views of the imposing mountain, Jebel Misht (left).

In these rugged mountains, just enough rain falls between December and March to support the growth of trees. Although the mountains are surrounded by barren desert with low shrubs, higher up the slopes these are replaced by olive and fig trees, then juniper woodland. Here it is cooler and there are more animals, including wild goats, gazelles and a few Arabian leopards, as well as many reptiles and birds.

Like all reptiles, blue-tailed Oman lizards sunbathe to warm up their blood.

Male shining sunbirds in their breeding plumage appear glossy in bright sunshine.

Sure-footed on rocky outcrops, the Arabian tahr is a kind of wild goat that lives in the mountains.

Immune to snake venom, honey badgers often kill and eat venomous snakes.

Glossary

abundant plentiful

ambush attack by surprise

amplify make louder

apex predator a predator at the top of the food chain

atoll coral island with a reef surrounding a lagoon

barren land with little or no vegetation

bask lie in the sun

broadleaved tree or plant with wide, flat leaves

conifer evergreen tree that produces cones and has needle-like leaves

coral reef a hard structure in the sea that is made from the remains of dead coral

creek a narrow inlet

crust Earth's outermost layer

crustaceans animals with an external skeleton, but no backbone, such as crabs

delta the area where a river drops its sediment as it enters a lake or the ocean

desert a place that receives little or no rainfall and has few plants or none at all

dormant not active, temporarily

echolocation working out the position of something by measuring the time taken for an echo to return

glacier a large body of ice moving slowly down a valley

krill shrimp-like marine animals

limestone sedimentary rock made of fossilised animal skeletons and shells

monsoon heavy seasonal rains in South Asia

peninsula a piece of land that is almost totally surrounded by water, but is not quite an island

pinnacle high, pointed piece of rock

plateau high, level ground

plumage birds' feathers

pollinate transfer pollen from one flower to another, so fertilising the second flower

predator an animal that hunts and kills other animals

prey animals that are eaten by other animals

sacred connected to a god or religion

snowmelt water that comes from melted snow

solitary alone

spatulate spoon-shaped (with a wide, rounded end)

thicket dense group of trees or bushes

tributary river or stream that flows into a larger river or a lake

tundra flat, treeless region of the Arctic where the ground is frozen for most of the year

venomous producing chemicals that can injure or kill prey

Books

Animal Families (series) by Tim Harris (Wayland, 2014)
Close-up Continents: Mapping Asia by Paul Rockett (Franklin Watts, 2016)
Infomojis: Continents by Jon Richards and Ed Simkins (Wayland, 2019)
Natural Wonders of the World by Molly Oldfield (Wren & Rook, 2019)

Websites

Asia Facts for Kids

Lots of interesting and fun facts on Asia.

www.kids-world-travel-guide.com/asia-facts.html

Geography for Kids

Has profiles of every country in Asia.

www.ducksters.com/geography/asia.php

Go Wild

Discover more about your favourite animals, including tigers,
in these WWF fact files.

gowild.wwf.org.uk/asia

National Geographic Animal Pictures and Facts

Simply type in the animals you're interested in, and get
lots of fascinating facts. Covers mammals, reptiles,
amphibians, fish and birds.

www.nationalgeographic.com/animals/index/

Note to parents and teachers: Every effort has been made by the Publishers to ensure that the websites in this book are of the highest educational value, and that they contain no inappropriate or offensive material. However, because of the nature of the Internet, it is impossible to guarantee that the contents of these sites will not be altered. We strongly advise that Internet access is supervised by a responsible adult.

Further information

Index